# CALL AND RESPONSE

# CALL AND RESPONSE

ELLA HABER
DAVID HABER

SAINT DUNSTAN'S PRESS

BALTIMORE, MARYLAND

Copyright © 2020 by Ella Haber & David Haber.

Illustrations and Photographs by Ella Haber.

All rights reserved. No part of this publication may be reproduced, distributed or transmitted in any form or by any means, including photocopying, recording, or other electronic or mechanical methods, without the prior written permission of the publisher, except in the case of brief quotations embodied in critical reviews and certain other noncommercial uses permitted by copyright law. For permission requests, write to the publisher, addressed "Attention: Permissions Coordinator," at the address below.

Saint Dunstan's Press
www.saintdunstanspress.com

Cover Design by Caleb Haber.

Call and Response / David Haber & Ella Haber – First Edition
ISBN (paperback) 978-0-9963237-7-2

# CONTENTS

Pain .................................................................................. 1

Chasing Pigeons ............................................................ 4

Listen .............................................................................. 8

The Lamp ..................................................................... 10

Woman ......................................................................... 12

Man ............................................................................... 14

Vermont ....................................................................... 16

The Green Mountains ................................................ 18

Silence .......................................................................... 20

One Chair .................................................................... 21

Invisible ....................................................................... 22

To the Cauldron ......................................................... 23

Age 12 .......................................................................... 24

Birthday ....................................................................... 25

Life, a Poem ................................................................ 28

Virtue ........................................................................... 29

What the Chair Has to Say ....................................... 30

What the TV Has to Say ............................................ 32

Expired ........................................................................ 34

Soured Milk ................................................................ 36

Night ............................................................................ 38

| | |
|---|---|
| The Pull | 40 |
| School | 42 |
| The Holy Trinity | 43 |
| Bragging | 46 |
| What We Show | 47 |
| The Fever | 48 |
| Woke | 51 |
| Fake Friends | 53 |
| Stitches | 56 |
| Freedom | 60 |
| Sand Castles | 64 |
| The Seed | 68 |

# DEDICATION

To us.

All of us.

Lost or found or wandering in the wilds of being a family.

# A DISCLAIMER

*From Ella:*

When I wrote these poems, I was twelve and emo AF 😢. Now I am fifteen and cool AF 😎. Oh. And wait until you see my art in the next book. 🎨

*From Dad:*
   Age twelve.
   That is when it happened to me. And that is when it happened to my daughter, Ella.
   So perhaps I should have known that poetry would slam her from all directions.
   We are not talking about the comforting couplets of Suess or the shape poems of kindergarten either. The emotional rawness of her adolescence was matched only by the naked feeling of music-wrapped words. Combine that with her finger itch to create, to draw, to write, to feel, to process, left me her dad in a pickle.
   How could I truly hear and feel her? How could I relate and remember? How could I respond to her call?
   How could we talk?

*Call and Response*

# PAIN

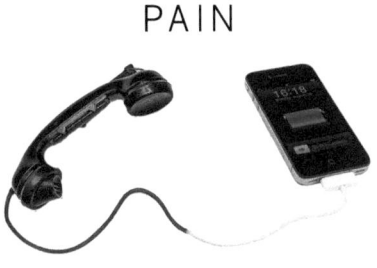

By Ella. H

I am sinking
Into the moist soil.
Wet words surround me,
Like a swarm of bees.
Each word is a sting.
I try to get out,
But it makes it worse.
I am a curse.
Drowning hurts.
I always lack
The urge to fight back.
I need to say something.
But words never escape
My dry mouth.
I try and just

Ignore,
But it makes me more
Torn.
Like ripped jeans
They say I'm so dark,
But who do you think
Turned off the lights?
They say my darkness is a sin,
But they are the monsters laying within.
Do I have love in my heart?
Am I the puzzle piece that is apart?
Is my spirit a criminal that's caught?
Am I known to be a person that just fought?
"I am a good person," is what I thought.
Apparently, I am not.
I am a child ready for a beatin'.
Feelin'
Like I am a president
That needs impeachin'.
Seein'
That I can't be myself.
It's a game,
And they're cheatin'.
Makin'
Me bleedin'
For needin'
Someone to feel me.
But all there is is a flock
Fleein'.

*Call and Response*

# CHASING PIGEONS

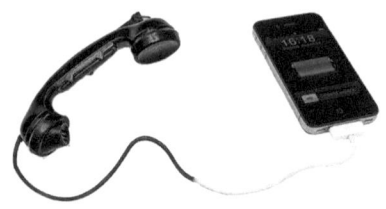

From Dad

A long time ago,
Ages it seems to me,
I, too, was young
But not free,
Just as you seem to be

Ripped and battered,
Words scattered,
Confidence shattered,
In tatters like your
Holey jeans.

And with memory backing
Toward my Winter
With those bluest of blue skies,
The chill air cracking,

*Call and Response*

*I remember*

*Sneakers too small;*
*Legs too tall; pants,*
*Too short, chant*
*With a corduroy*
*Swish-swish.*

*Hundreds of pigeons*
*Painting a religion*
*Of color,*
*A glimpse of iridescent blue*
*Among the plumed*

*White and black and gray*
*A flock waiting.*
*Friends. Please stay.*
*I have bread crumbed*
*A gift to be passed with numbed*

*Fingers and thumbs*
*If only they stay*
*And they wait.*
*They wait.*
*They stay.*

*Swish. Swish.*

Ella & David Haber

*I chase and with a snap*
*Feathers crack and flap.*
*My flock flees*
*With me on bruised knees*
*Crumbs extended between*

*Fingers and thumbs —*
*Numb —*
*Like my frozen tongue*
*And words never come*
*Except to taunt*

*My memory with what-ifs*
*And what-nots*
*And those unspoken words*
*Are the only flock*
*I have remaining of*

*My Winter shaming:*
*My silenced words,*
*Spoken never,*
*Ever. Except now, dear.*
*To recast, the past with a spring made clear.*

# LISTEN

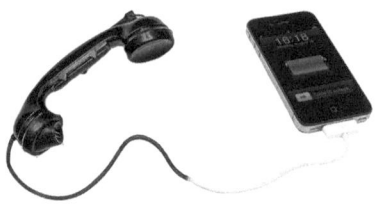

By Ella. H


Listen
Listen to my wishes
Listen to me
You listen to each other
I'm not your mother
I'm not your father
I'm not your lover
But I am your child
I have wishes, too
And you don't have a clue
You don't listen
You don't respect my wishes
Sure, you aren't a genie in a bottle
But you are my goddamn model
You don't listen

*Call and Response*

Late at night
When I hear your voices
You don't give a crap
But when I speak my mind
You just laugh
Look through my eyes
See my cries and hear
Listen
Listen to my wishes
Listen.

# THE LAMP

From Dad



*How brash —*
*This burnished brass*
*With wick twinkling bright*
*In the mature quiet of night.*

*So loud with light!*

*How this lamp glows!*
*And sadly shows*
*The wide world is not*
*Fair — justice an afterthought.*

*So very loud with light!*

*You are, or course, right.*
*But without a genie in sight*
*Wishes are but wishes*
*And a child's eye misses*

## Call and Response

*The model of our whispered light,*

*Subdued, but shining bright.*
*When viewed from age's height,*
*One sees eyelashes kiss*
*Cherub cheeks with a wish —*
*By soft light —*

*Of Good Night.*

# WOMAN

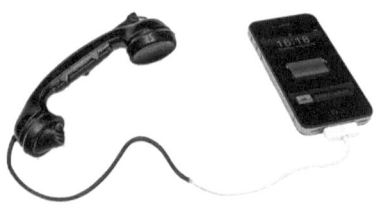

By Ella. H

Woman,
Known to be
The gender that couldn't.
We want to fight;
He tells us we shouldn't!
He says:
    We didn't do that.
Well, the proof
Is in the puddin'.
If someone tells us
To watch
While they play
Soccer,
We wouldn't!
They insult us,
Our work.

*Call and Response*

They don't know
Our effort.
So how about
They shut up!
For once.
They need to
Listen to us
Because — duh — we are

# MAN

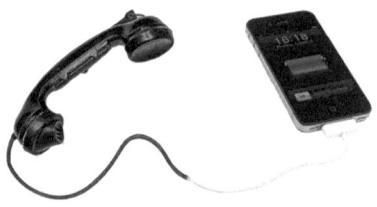

From Dad


Man,
We didn't do that.
Now that is what we say
With wrinkled words each day.
But with the dumb power
Of our bodies — those towers
Resembling macho sunflowers
Reaching
Toward the light —
Do we rightly empower?

Or rather, out of sight,
Do we, with each passing hour,
Cause her to sour
And rot in the shade
From shadows betrayed

## Call and Response

*By our very reaching —*
*Shadows that harass,*
*That degrade,*
*And make her afraid?*
*Listen!*
*Hear, the wail beseeching:*
   *#MeToo*
*Shouted at the light.*
*Don't talk.*
*Listen,*
*Man.*

# VERMONT

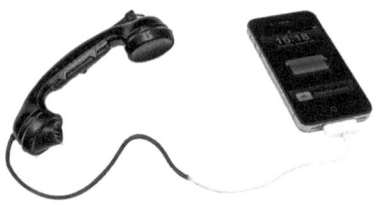

By Ella. H

I think of that day.
Three months past May.
It was not a very great week, I must say.
Could it have ended in a "hip-hip-hooray?
It didn't —
So yay!
Not.
The whole week, I was wiping away snot.
If my life was a movie,
It would have a devastating plot.
My heart felt like I had been shot;
My thoughts were in a knot;
My soul was like an empty parking lot.
Do you know how I feel now?
Probably not —

*Call and Response*

"Knock, knock."

"Heart? Are you coming out?"

"Are you still there?"

"Yes. In a while.
Just to be fair.
Your friends did something to me
Without any care.
They broke me,
And left a tear."

## THE GREEN MOUNTAINS

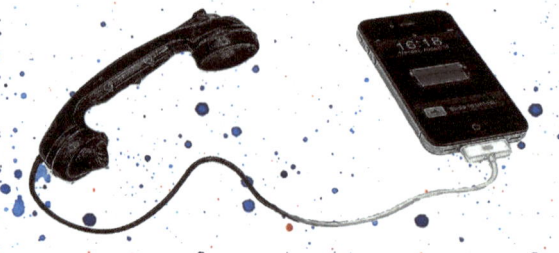

From Dad.

Once, many moons ago, the earth shifted –
Like a restless man in unstable sleep
Crashing and waking – bedrock uplifted,
Chipped rock raised in heavenly reaching heaps.

Stone fingers, new formed, with digits clifted
And jagged, rent the midnight dark down deep –
Keeping even the stars dimmed, light pitted,
Broken by the sudden mountainous sleep.

Rain and wind and the passing sun gifted
Us with gray grit and golden glows that seep
And erode bleak crags, now recommitted
To grasping roots in soil deep that keeps
      The once barren and broken mountains green
      And pulls the torn heart from Vermont's ravine.

*Call and Response*

# SILENCE

By Ella. H

I can't stand it —
When I'm nobody to everybody.
My words are dissolved by the air.
My feelings just gum on your shoes.
I'm always just ...
There
Wait —
I forgot.
Nobody cares.
Will my funeral have only one chair?

*Call and Response*

# ONE CHAIR

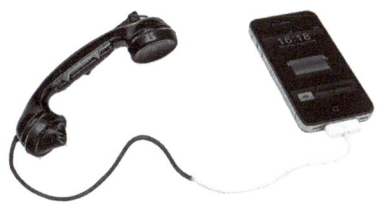

From Dad

*Our lives are music
That plays and plays and plays
Through bright nights and dark days.
Until
It doesn't and all that remains
Is a single chair,
Where once we sat
Sometimes like a drunk cat
Awash in midwinter sun —
Sometimes like an anxious fan, ahum
As the seconds tick and the buzzer blare
With electric dreams
Of new hope and fantastic love.
Someday all our music will stop.
The game eventually ends.
The chair is empty. And sends
All who glance into a reverie
Of sad stares as the worn seat bends
With the ghost of rending memories caught
In the echo of music done.*

# INVISIBLE

By Ella. H

My mom always told me
To crawl out of my solid shell,
To step out of my bubble of fear.
But, frankly,
Bubbles are sometimes hard to pop.
I want to be important.
I want to actually talk.
But there's always
That red sign in my way
Shouting, "STOP!"
I'm an onion
But the chef's already going
Chop. Chop. Chop.
I don't want my life wasted
But it feels like it's already
In the trash can.
Maybe I could climb from this fire
To the pan.

*Call and Response*

## TO THE CAULDRON

From Dad

*A turtle chews gum*
*With a double bubble shell*
*Toil. Trouble. Talk!*

## AGE 12

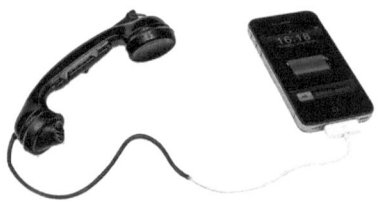

By Ella. H

Everyone thinks I'm 9.
Yes,
I'm short.
And that's just fine.
But, if you're going to say something about me,
Look inside.
You can try to put Band-Aids on scratches,
But you can't fix mine.
They ask me if I'm fine.
I say:
"Yes."
I lie.
They say I'm smart and mature
But wait,
I thought I was 9.

*Call and Response*

# BIRTHDAY

From Dad

*Wisdom comes in all sizes.
It is not awarded through prizes
As the days pass
And candles are fast
Extinguished by puffed breath
Bursting with wishes unspoken.*

*Rather it is seen by eyes soaking
In openness and wonder –
That unblinding thunder
Of pure feeling felt as an other,
Sister as brother, father as mother,
Human as human together.*

*Neither size nor age holds
Wisdom's bright keys.
It is the eyes
With heart vision that molds –
That fights and pries
Us forward. And up*

*Above the waxed candle and frosted cake
With smoke curling wishes toward Heaven's gate.*

# LIFE, A POEM

By Ella. H

What is the point of life?
I am asking because clearly
I can't figure out that riddle.
  What is the point of being
  Loved, if you're just going to
    Die in the end? I mean, let's
    Be honest, I love life but some
      Times it is cruel. It's a Love /
      Hate relationship. Me and Life, we ...
      We are like a middle-aged couple.
      Let's just say we don't always get
      Along.

*Call and Response*

# VIRTUE

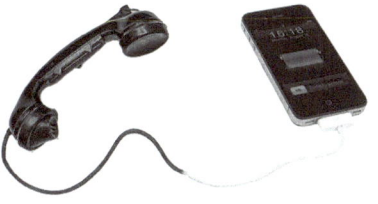

From Dad

*Once there was an ancient philosopher,
Who, like a rolling stone, would not suffer
Moss growing on the pebble of his mind
In the quest to find reason behind
This scrabble of humankind we call life.
His friends would say: All is flux. All is strife.*

*Maybe so — but how to know, he wondered.
Many questions formed to pull asunder
His once unexamined, now roiling, soul.
Each query pulling closer to the goal
Of Truth found curled in the hooked question mark
Of Life. But that stark arc is always dark*

*Like fast Achilles chasing a turtle
Caught betwixt the here and the Eternal.*

## WHAT THE CHAIR HAS TO SAY

By Ella. H

I try to hold her up
But her thought pushes me down.
Her realization
Forces me to be patient.
I just want to break
But I keep holding up
Her body that's shakin'.
I could hear the thought
Coming into her brain
Like a train in a subway station.
I tried to cushion the new seeds of
The plantation,
But the pieces to her shooting thoughts
Were stars
Already forming a constellation.
I wish I could talk.

*Call and Response*

I wish I could tell her
That it's not a bad thing
That the workers on her railway
Never
Go on vacation.

## WHAT THE TV HAS TO SAY

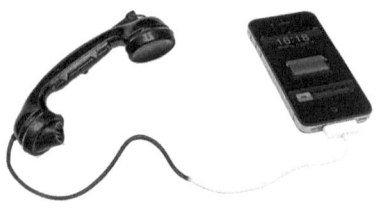

From Dad

I can't control my voice
I have no choice
Words just tumble and stumble,
Sometimes loudly, sometimes a mumble
But never my words.
And my face — oh my poor face
Flickering and flashing
At an uncontrolled pace
With a movement and emotion
Not my own.
With a click, I'm happy.
With a flick, I'm sappy.
Now sad. Now mad.
Back again, and now glad.
Stop. Please just stop.
Let me see what I am,
Who I am, I mean. Damn.

*Call and Response*

*Gimme silence. Gimme the peace
Of being the black screen above
The mantelpiece.*

# EXPIRED

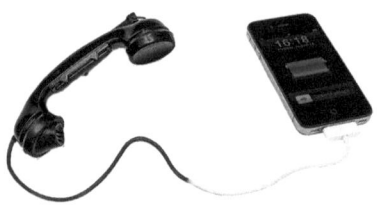

By Ella. H

I open my fridge
And remember
All those expiration dates.
They don't last forever.
January 7.
March 11.
You never know when your life will
Expire.
Each day, we get eaten.
Little by little.
Their words take away ours,
The sounds like
Honking cars.
Then the day comes.
It has become enough.
The perfect white milk

Starts to curdle.
The apples
Begin to shrivel.
Each day we hope to ignore the bullies.
We really try.
But it isn't enough.
The time is up
And we die.

# SOURED MILK

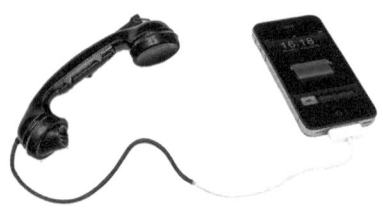

From Dad


Milk pressed by Time's passing,
Left like dried pulp amassing
As juice is extracted
To leave once proud fruit rejected,
Sits on the kitchen counter —
As chunky as New England chowder.

A sinking, subtle, sickening scent
Wafting in the bright morning air, went
Straight in the nostrils, to flare
The brain with a double dare
Not to gag and retch
As we catch our breath.

Wasted again. Useless —
Unless we shift and wrest
A recipe from our limited minds
And find a purpose for the forgotten rinds —
That fibrous fruit garbage — and milk bubbled
And soured leaving us with a breakfast troubled.

Hmmmmmmmm. Mmmmmmmmm.
Apple buttermilk pancakes anyone?

## Call and Response

# NIGHT

By Ella. H

When the bright sun sets,
The colors of the world go.
They disappear. Poof.

When the bright sun sets,
The beauty of the world dims
Casting a shadow.

When the bright sun sets,
The world sleeps, creating death
And screams in the night.

When the bright sun sets,
Darkness falls, but the moon jumps.
Two colors combine.

When the bright sun sets,
We try to forget our past.
Like suns, thoughts come back.

Call and Response

# THE PULL

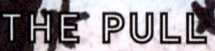

The moon and sun are in a race
Each orbiting with blinding color
Painting Heaven and Earth and Water in a chase
Of fired light, one reflecting the other.

Circles and circles and circles again
Marking time, bending sky toward twilight
Watched by billions and billions from a starry den.
The orange-yellow Day and blue-dark Night

Touching but twice a cycle spun
Neither leading, 'til gravity has won.

# SCHOOL

By Ella. H

### BACKPACKS
My turquoise backpack,
It lays there like a blank page.
Useless but useful.

### BOOKS
There's so many books.
They lay on a flat canvas.
What's in their pages?

### CORKBOARDS
I feel bad for you,
You have to get pricked with sharp
Points. Everyday

# THE HOLY TRINITY

From Dad

*Backpacks, books, and corkboards.*
*Backpacks, books, and corkboards.*
*That holy trinity of learning:*
*Openness, curiosity, and empathy flirting*

*And flitting together like butterflies*
*Carry wisdom to color our skies*
*With their rainbowed wings –*
*Those stitched delicate strings*
*That sing if we but listen*
*So let us reposition*
*Ourselves.*

*With openness, curiosity, and empathy*
*Next to those*
*Backpacks, books, and corkboards.*
                      *Our backpacks, books, and corkboards.*

# BRAGGING

By Ella. H

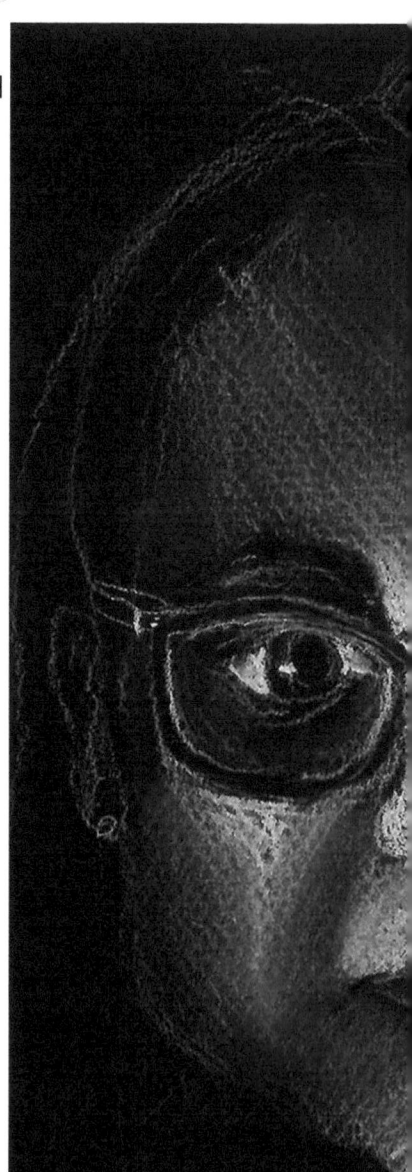

I'm too good at everything,
Or at least I say so.
Truthfully,
I'm not.
I don't actually think that.
These thoughts
Overfill my brain:
That *I'm* not as good as them.
And that I'm just ... a ... well —
Plane Jane.
It's called jealousy.
I get overwhelmed by the fact that
They're better than me.
They say I'm "modest"
Sarcastically.

*Call and Response*

# WHAT WE SHOW

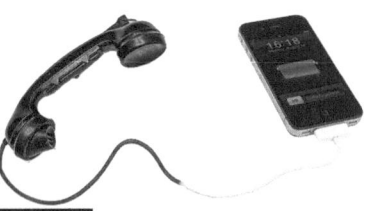

From Dad

    *The crown makes the queen;*
    *Camo makes the marine;*
    *Overalls make the farmer;*
    *The tuxedo makes the charmer.*
    *We are what we wear*
    *Because that is what we share,*
    *Out there, in the world,*
    *Truth with fiction swirled.*

    *Mixed, dissolved, unified*
*Into a melted thing called me, applied*
    *Inside and outside both*
    *Sworn by my whispered troth.*
*Mapped by my every outward action made*
*And every thought thunk in the shade,*
    *The inside is out*
    *And the outside is in*

*And somewhere in the middle is me.*

# THE FEVER

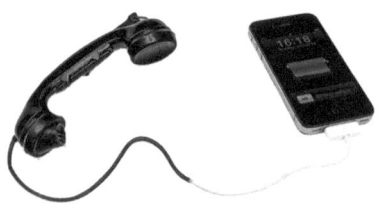

By Ella. H

I think I have a fever.
My armpits are sweating.
My hands are shaking.
I think I have a fever.

And, Dad, I'm not faking.

My face is red.
I need some meds.
I kinda wanna be dead.
Dad, I think I have a fever.

I'm hot and cold.
My heart's up for sale —
Cha-ching. Sold!
I feel like I'm drowning.

I know, Dad, I'm sounding
Crazy.
But, I think I have a fever.

*Call and Response*

I'm burning
Up so fast.
I'm learning
Never to react
To the world again
I think I have a fever.

Somebody once said:
"Keep on walking."
But what if my path is cracking
And every step I take
My soul breaks.
For God's sake,
I think I have a fever.

My tongue feels dry.
There's no tears left to cry;
No funeral when I die.
I really think I have a fever.

I'm banging on the door.
I can feel the warmth
Inside.
Someone please let me in.
Even if I have a fever,
Don't leave me in the dark.

Just another of my fears,
I know. I'm no Shakespeare,
But I, at least, want to appear
To be someone.

We were supposed to be
The 3 Musketeers.
But I might as well disappear.
Please, guys, open the door.
It's cold out here.

*Call and Response*

# WOKE

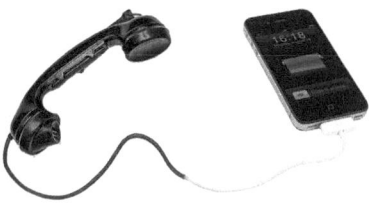

From Dad

*At night, among the stars,*
*Or below the stars, or maybe*
*There are no stars,*
*I sleep and dream*

*Or rather I should be*
*Sleeping and dreaming.*
*But instead,*
*PJS are soaked;*
*Skin is sticky,*
*Clammy. Hot.*
*No. Cold.*
*No.*

*Whatever.*
*That night spider came again;*
*Drenched me*
*With his stinky moist*
*Breath.*
*But I, too, am hot and wet*
*And alone*
*Drowning in a midnight sweat.*

*Call and Response*

# FAKE FRIENDS

By Ella. H

Every time I look at you
My heart sinks like the Titanic.
Every time I think of you I
Become apoplectic.
Every time I hear you, my eyes
Swell up.
They could fill the Atlantic.

My heart a frozen iceberg.

Or maybe I'm like air.
It goes unnoticed
I have no meaning
I have no motive

No air.

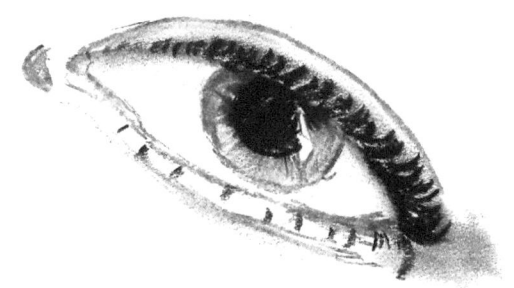

I drowned.
Everyone else floated;
I'm a shadow.

I was never sugar-coated.
I get you don't like me.
Got it. Noted.
How?
How can your best friends ditch you?

You dumped me in a trash can —
Left me all alone
And not with a drop of regret?
It's like I'm a stinky cologne.

Ella Haber: the girl whose best
Friends ditched her.
My soul stings like blisters.
You were my sisters!
Now my name comes out your mouth
In whispers.
As I write this,
You talk behind my back.
It feels like
Hatred.
It feels like an
Attack.

Your soul's dark.
Your soul's black.
Bitches.

# STITCHES

From Dad

*Layers of skin parted*
*Throbbing, pulsing, heart*
*Pumping, eyes dilated and darting*
*With shock and pain: a parting,*
*Rending all that was.*

*Friendship tattered and torn*
*A teenage wasteland to mourn*
*Not even the happy horn*
*Of summer new born*
*Numbs life, sundered.*

*Memories have been plundered.*
*Every good moment, painted black*
*And hacked*
*To bits.*
*Smaller and smaller.*

*Call and Response*

*Until nothing remains*

*But a wound. Growinggrowinggrowinggrowinggrowing growingandgrowingandgrowingandgrowingandgrowingandgrowingandgrowingandgrowingandgrowingandgrowingandgrowingandgrowingandgrowingandgrowingandgrowingandgrowingandgrowingandgrowingandgrowingandgrowingandgrowingandgrowingandgrowingandgrowingandgrowingandgrowingandgrowingandgrowingandgrowingandgrowingandgrowingandgrowingandgrowingandgrowingandgrowingandgrowingand*

GROWING

Those bitches.
They are the ones in need of stitches.
Those broken little bitches.
Get the thread.
Let's sew.
Together.

# FREEDOM

By Ella. H

I sometimes wish I were the
Only person alive
That everyone else didn't survive
And that it was just me and
The sky
I sometimes wish I didn't have
Pains like cavities;
That there were no taxes and salaries
And that nothing was pulling me
Down except for gravity
I would just lay there on
The ground
Letting the world spin 'round and
'Round
The breeze would sweep my anxiety
Away
The stars keeping me forever

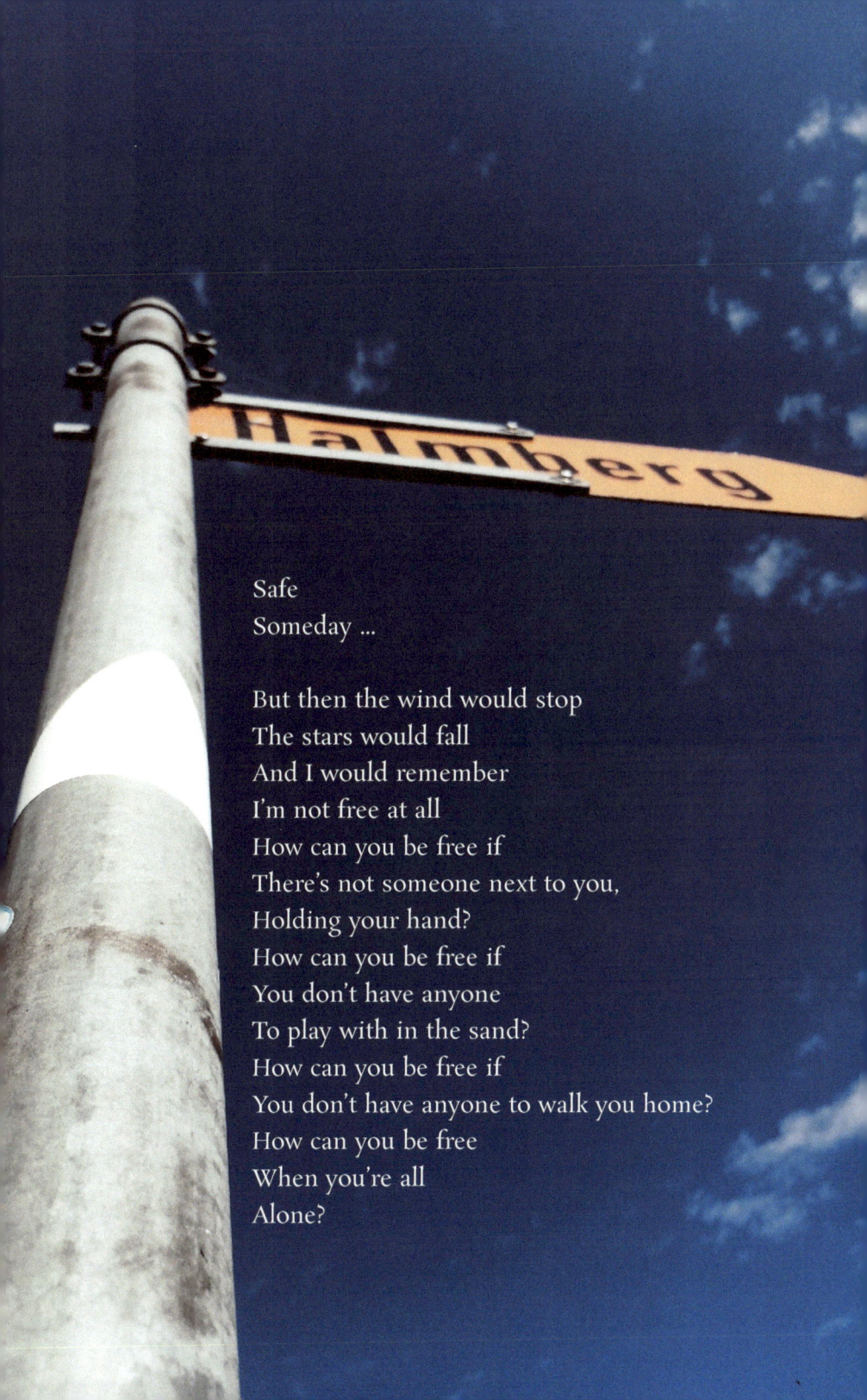

Safe
Someday ...

But then the wind would stop
The stars would fall
And I would remember
I'm not free at all
How can you be free if
There's not someone next to you,
Holding your hand?
How can you be free if
You don't have anyone
To play with in the sand?
How can you be free if
You don't have anyone to walk you home?
How can you be free
When you're all
Alone?

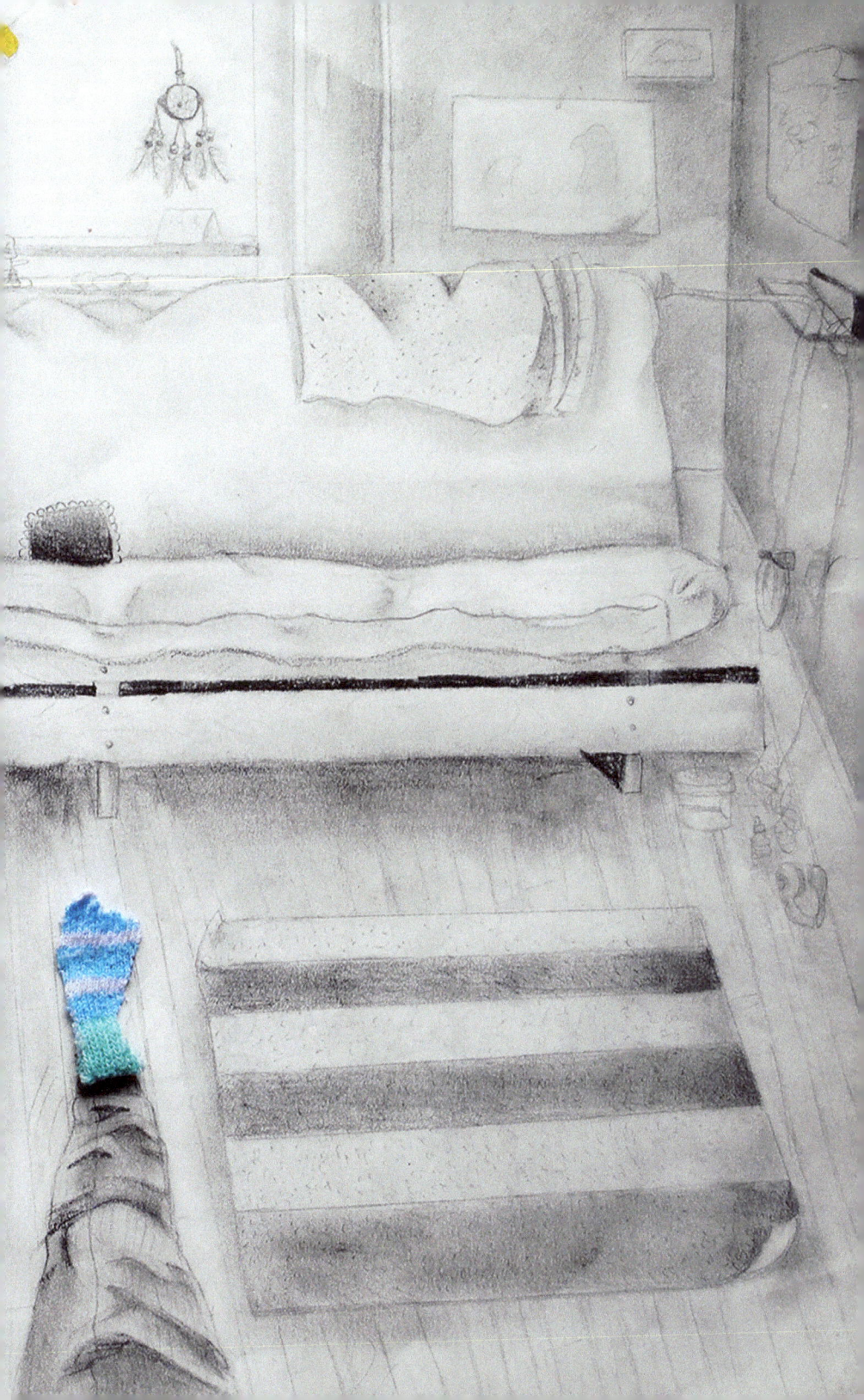

# SAND CASTLES

From Dad

*There is the sand.*
*There are the pails.*
*There are the shovels.*
*There are the sifters.*
*There are the rakes.*
*And there are the molds,*
*Shaped like shells and snails.*
*Perhaps that will be a moat,*
*That mound a wall,*
*That hole,*
*A tunnel to dungeons most foul.*

*But here. Right here*
*Is the trail.*
*Here.*
*Take my hand.*
*You shall not fail.*

# Call and Response

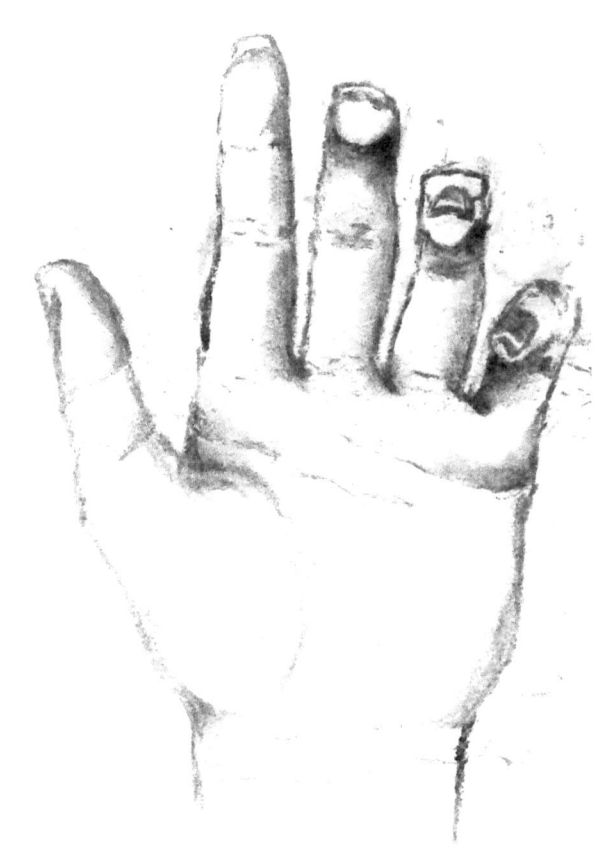

# THE SEED

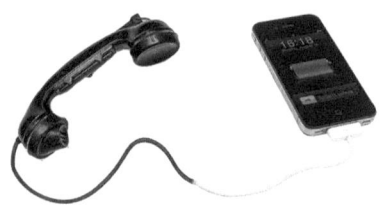

By Ella. H

I am a seed.
My parents planted me in the ground when
I was young.
They patted the dirt around me down,
hoping, praying no one would stomp on me.
I guess they jinxed it.
You see,
I was growing, a little slowly, but still
growing.
Little green leaves poked from my stem;
they were soft and bright.
But then one day, this gust of wind
came, and knocked one of my leaves off.
It was okay though because I learned
to grow it back, a bit harder, and more
camouflaged.

*Call and Response*

Years passed and I grew beautiful yellow
petals, with blue designs in them,
but that's when things changed.
One day, bugs crawled up my stem,
and started to chew through it.
Luckily I learned to grow thorns.
Another day, a dog came up and tried
digging up my roots!
Thankfully, for me, I grew thicker,
stronger roots, so they wouldn't
break.
Another day, furious winds came and
blew all my petals
off.
Luckily for me, I learned that looks
don't matter; I don't really need petals.
More recently, one kid came by
and stepped on me!
Awesome for me.
Even though my stem was broken
my roots were still there,
the seed of me was, too.
I learned to grow back.
A few months ago a drought started,
gusts of sand are flung at me.
I haven't had water in weeks.

My leaves are wilting,
my petals are colorless;
in fact most are gone.
I think I am dying again.

But, still I am a seed!
I just have to grow back.
One. More. Time.

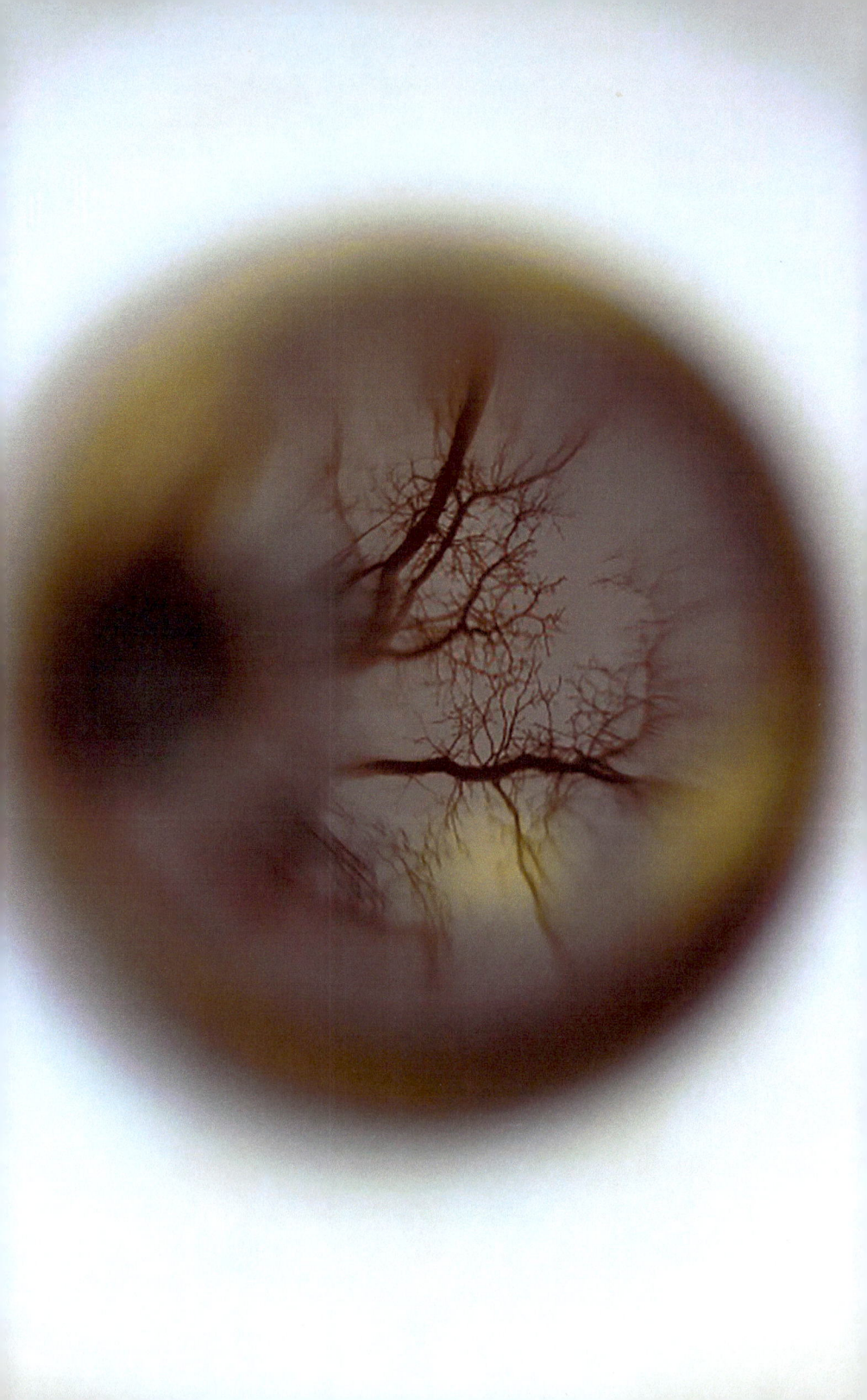

www.ingramcontent.com/pod-product-compliance
Lightning Source LLC
Chambersburg PA
CBHW041508010526
44118CB00006B/189